BEASTS AND THE BATTLEFIELD

BEASTLY FIREPOWER

MILITARY WEAPONS AND TACTICS INSPIRED BY ANIMALS

Lisa M. Bolt Simons

CAPSTONE PRESS
a capstone imprint

Captivate is published by Capstone Press, an imprint of Capstone
1710 Roe Crest Drive, North Mankato, Minnesota 56003
www.capstonepub.com

Copyright © 2020 by Capstone. All rights reserved. No part of this publication may be reproduced in whole or in part, or stored in a retrieval system, or transmitted in any form or by any means, electronic, mechanical, photocopying, recording, or otherwise, without written permission of the publisher

Library of Congress Cataloging-in-Publication Data
Names: Simons, Lisa M. B., 1969- author.
Title: Beastly firepower : military weapons and tactics inspired by animals / Lisa M. Bolt Simons.
Other titles: Military weapons and tactics inspired by animals
Description: North Mankato : Capstone Press, 2020. | Series: Beasts and the battlefield | Includes bibliographical references and index. | Audience: Grades 4-6 | Audience: Ages 8-11 | Summary: "In the wild, animals use teeth, claws, and other natural weapons to attack their prey. On the battlefield, soldiers need weapons to fight the enemy. Military forces have often looked to nature for inspiration to develop effective weapons and combat tactics. From the first feathered arrows to tomorrow's high-tech weaponry, take a look at how military technology often imitates the natural weapons of animals to help soldiers succeed in combat. Then be sure to catch the other amazing titles in the Beasts and the Battlefield series"— Provided by publisher.
Identifiers: LCCN 2019045429 (print) | LCCN 2019045430 (ebook) | ISBN 9781543590227 (hardcover) | ISBN 9781496665928 (paperback) | ISBN 9781543590272 (pdf)
Subjects: LCSH: Military weapons—Juvenile literature. | Military art and science—Technological innovations—Juvenile literature. | Biomimicry—Juvenile literature.
Classification: LCC UF500 .S555 2020 (print) | LCC UF500 (ebook) | DDC 623.4—dc23
LC record available at https://lccn.loc.gov/2019045429
LC ebook record available at https://lccn.loc.gov/2019045430

Editorial Credits
Aaron Sautter, editor; Kyle Grenz, designer; Morgan Walters, media researcher; Katy LaVigne, production specialist

Image Credits
Alamy: AB Forces News Collection, bottom 21, bottom 27, CPC Collection, top 19, Dudley Little, 15, Hum Images, bottom right 24; Newscom: Pacific Press/Sipa USA, top left 26; Shutterstock: aapsky, top 29, Ana Gram, bottom left 24, Andrea Izzotti, bottom 9, Artistdesign29, design element throughout, Artur Tiutenko, 4, Benny Marty, 20, Chesky, 23, Christian Musat, middle 21, Elenarts, top 9, Eric Isselee, middle right 14, Everett Historical, top right 11, Fasttailwind, bottom 11, Gallinago_media, middle 18, Glass and Nature, 6, Henrik Larsson, bottom right 12, iurii, bottom 18, Joerg Huettenhoelscher, 7, KASIRA SUDA, bottom right 13, Kbiros, top 17, klptgrph, bottom right cover, Laura Dinraths, 25, Manbetta, middle 27, maxtimofeev, bottom left 12, moosehenderson, 10, MRS. SUCHARUT CHOUNYOO, 5, Omelchenko, design element throughout, Ondrej Prosicky, bottom 29, Panaiotidi, top 20, PetlinDmitry, bottom left 14, photovova, top right 26, Piotr Wawrzyniuk, bottom spread 16-17, Protasov AN, 22, Red Squirrel, bottom left 8, Sanit Fuangnakhon, middle 8, Sergey Kamshylin, bottom left 13, bottom left 28, THE PICTURE RESEARCHER, bottom right 28, Thorsten Spoerlein, top left cover, Will Thomass, middle 19

All internet sites appearing in back matter were available and accurate when this book was sent to press.

Printed in the United States   5451

Table of Contents

Superior Weapons in the Animal World **4**

Imitation Drives History **8**

Copying Nature for Today's Weapons **14**

Beastly Weapons of the Future **22**

> Glossary 30
> Read More 31
> Internet links 31
> Index 32

Words in **bold** are in the glossary.

Superior Weapons in the Animal World

More than 100 years ago, the air was filled with a terrifying sound. Nearly 400 British tanks rumbled onto the battlefield. On November 20, 1917, the tanks defeated German troops in France. Tanks were new weapons in World War I (1914–1918). They could climb steep hills and roll through fences. They fired big guns as they charged the enemy.

British WWI tank

Tanks are big and powerful. But in some ways, they are like centipedes. These small **predators** can easily crawl over rocks, sticks, and leaves. They also attack **prey** with natural weapons. Humans make many deadly weapons. But nature made its own weapons first.

centipede

Following Nature's Lead

Copying animals to make new inventions is called **biomimicry**. Inventors have followed nature's example for thousands of years. More than 2,000 years ago, a scientist named Archytas [AR-key-tus] made a mechanical dove. It wasn't a weapon. But it helped future inventors think about copying animal features.

Throughout history, people have tried to copy animals to make weapons. Today's armies still look to nature. From bows and arrows to today's vehicles, animals often spark ideas for new kinds of weapons.

Helicopters can hover in one place like hummingbirds.

FACT
The word "biomimicry" comes from two ancient Greek words. *Bios* means "life," and *mimesis* means "to imitate" or copy.

Imitation Drives History

Long ago, fighters probably didn't know their weapons borrowed from nature. But without animals, their weapons wouldn't have worked very well.

Bows and arrows were invented more than 70,000 years ago. But arrows didn't fly well at first. Then people began putting bird feathers on arrows. Feathers are strong and flexible. They help arrows spin and fly straight to their target.

Goose feathers helped the first arrows fly straight.

Ancient ships often rammed other ships in battle. Some ships had strong, curved **prows** covered in bronze metal. Others had long poles called bowsprits sticking out from the front. These ramming ships acted like how a dolphin attacks enemies. Dolphins sometimes ram sharks with their strong noses.

Curved prows on ships were strong like a dolphin's nose.

FACT
Dolphins attack by ramming into a shark's belly. This stuns the shark or knocks it out. Sometimes these hard blows may even kill a shark.

Flying Toward the Future

A little more than 100 years ago, Orville and Wilbur Wright studied birds. They saw how the shape of a bird's wings helped it fly. The brothers decided to copy nature's design. They built the first powered, fixed-wing airplane.

Armies soon learned that airplanes could be used in battle. Since World War I, there have been many types of military planes. Today's bombers and fighter planes carry many weapons. They can attack targets on land or fight other planes. But these planes wouldn't fly at all if birds didn't do it first.

Early model of the Wright brothers airplane before WWI

bomber plane

fighter plane

Small but Powerful

Some ideas for weapons come from tiny animals. Tortoise beetle **larvae** make shields from their own poop! They carry it over their backs. If an attacker approaches, the beetle swings the poop shield at it. Long ago, soldiers sometimes used their shields in the same way. Spartan warriors bashed enemies with shields to knock them out or kill them.

Tortoise beetle larvae attack enemies with their poop shields like Spartan warriors.

Running, Jumping Tanks

In the late 1940s scientists tried making new kinds of tanks. They designed tanks that could run like horses or jump like grasshoppers. Small models were built. But tanks were too big and heavy to copy the animal's movements. The idea was dropped.

In more recent wars, soldiers often used flamethrowers. These weapons could burn targets up to 65 feet (20 meters) away. They worked a lot like a bombardier beetle's natural weapon. The beetle shoots hot chemicals from its backside. The chemicals reach about 212 degrees Fahrenheit (100 degrees Celsius).

Copying Nature for Today's Weapons

Today's weapons also copy animal **traits**. Several animals use chemical weapons. When threatened, skunks can spray a strong-smelling chemical at enemies. They can hit targets up to 10 feet (3 m) away. The powerful smell can last for days.

Some smaller creatures also use chemical weapons. The 3-inch (7.6-centimeter) whip scorpion uses acid. It squirts the burning liquid from its backside to scare away enemies.

skunk

whip scorpion

FACT
The spitting spider lives up to its name—it spits! It attacks by spitting sticky silk. The strands of silk tie down its prey. The silk is made in the spider's **venom glands**.

Armed forces also use chemicals. They use pepper spray as a nonlethal weapon. The chemicals sting people's skin and eyes. It's so strong that enemies often give up without a fight.

Police officers sometimes use pepper spray to control dangerous crowds.

Going Electric

Tasers are another nonlethal weapon. When fired, two **electrodes** shoot out on wires. Electricity then zaps the target. The person is usually stunned for a short time.

Electric eels also stun targets with electricity. They have organs with special cells. The cells store power like batteries. The eels use this power in two ways. They can search for prey using a low-level charge. But if an eel is attacked, it jolts the enemy with a blast of power. An electric eel's shock is about ten times stronger than a Taser gun.

Tasers and electric eels both use electricity to stun enemies.

Using Invisible Light

Soldiers sometimes look for enemies at night or from great distances. Gear based on nature helps them. People can't see **infrared** light. But we can feel it. The warmth of the sun comes from infrared light. Mosquitoes use infrared to track their warm-blooded prey. U.S. Navy submarines use infrared sensors. Like the mosquito, the sensors help find and track warm targets.

Military radar planes can find targets like a falcon's eyes can spot prey.

Most birds of prey have excellent sight. A falcon can see prey almost 2 miles (3 kilometers) away. The E-8C Joint STARS plane can also find distant targets. Using **radar**, it can find targets more than 155 miles (250 km) away. The information helps troops know where to attack.

The Power of Sound

Animals such as bats, dolphins, and some whales use **echolocation**. They make clicking and whistling sounds. The sound waves bounce off insects or fish and return to the animals. They can tell how close food is based on the echoes.

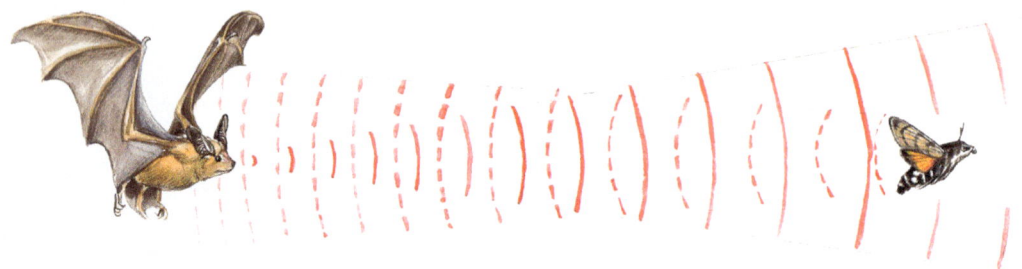

Dolphin Guard Duty

During the Vietnam War (1954–1975), the U.S. Navy trained dolphins to act as guards. Dolphins used echolocation to find enemy divers. Once found, a dolphin then attached a special device to a diver. The device then filled with air. This forced the enemy to the surface where he could be captured.

This skill is copied by several **sonic** weapons. One is the Long Range Acoustic Device (LRAD). Its powerful beams of sound can target enemies nearly 2 miles (3 km) away. The LRAD can cause painful headaches or make people feel sick. Enemies often run away when hit with the loud sounds.

orca whale

LRAD

Beastly Weapons of the Future

Scientists continue to study animals and what they can do. They keep inventing new weapons based on what they learn. The future of military weapons could be limitless.

Most insects are quite small. But many have amazing features. For example, the surface of a moth's eyes is special. Light doesn't shine off of them. Inventors hope to copy this feature to make new anti-radar equipment. Airplanes could appear completely invisible to enemies.

Insects, birds, and fish often gather in swarms. In the future, robots may be used in **aerial** swarms. A swarm could be 250 or more small unmanned aircraft called **drones**. These swarms could overpower targets. Like a swarm of bees, they may attack from many directions. Bees swarm together to chase away enemies.

Swarms of military drones may one day attack enemy fighters like swarms of bees.

Pershing II missile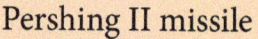

Longer-Range Weapons

Migrating birds are able to find their way over long distances. Sensors in missiles help guide them to hit distant targets. Scientists hope to make sensors that work more like a bird's sense of direction. The new sensors will be stronger and more accurate.

New sensors will act like a bird's natural sense of direction to help guide missiles.

migrating geese

electric ray

Tasers are useful weapons. However, their wires are only 15 feet (4.6 m) long. Future Tasers may use electric bullets instead. Bullets could reach targets more than 325 feet (99 m) away. They will also **paralyze** targets for up to three minutes. Electric rays, or torpedo fish, attack in a similar way. They shoot out a strong burst of electricity to stun their prey.

SpotMini robot

German Shepherd

Droids as Weapons

What do you think future weapons will be like? If you thought of robots, you aren't alone. Many scientists are working on animal-like robots.

One model is called SpotMini. It is about the size of a large dog. It can run like a dog for about 90 minutes. It has an arm that can pick up objects or open doors. In the future, robots like SpotMini may be armed with weapons. They may even replace troops on the battlefield.

Scientists are also working on micro aerial vehicles (MAVs). These robots are as small as dragonflies. One day they may be as tiny as mosquitoes. They could be the perfect spies. Micro robots could inject targets with tiny tracking devices. They could also shoot poison into enemies on the battlefield.

Animal-Inspired Firepower

Nature has perfected animals' weapons over millions of years. Armies have long tried to copy them. From feathered arrows to high-tech robots, many weapons have copied animal abilities.

The armed forces owe much of their success to nature. Without animal-based weapons, troops may not succeed in battle. Soldiers will likely face new challenges in the future. Nature will provide ideas for new inventions to meet them. Future weapons will be stronger, faster, and more powerful—all thanks to animals.

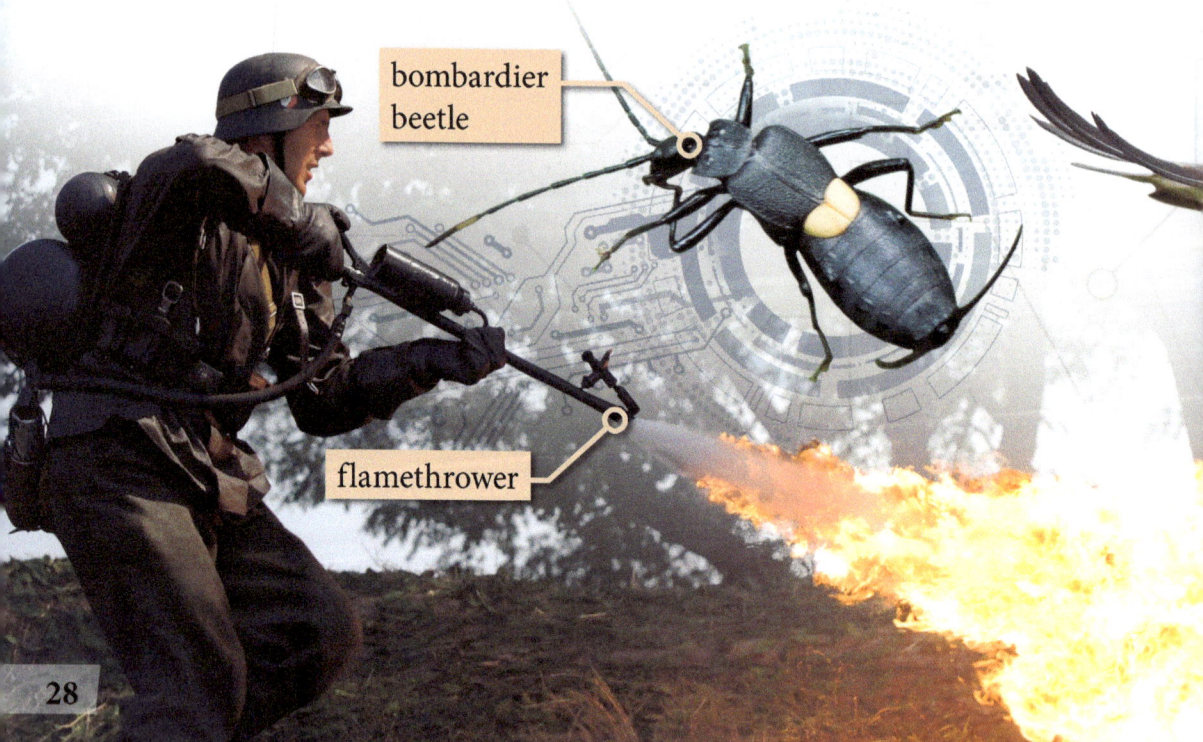

Glossary

aerial (AYR-ee-uhl)—relating to something that happens in the air

biomimicry (by-oh-MIM-mih-kree)—copying the design of a living thing

drone (DROHN)—an unmanned, remote-controlled aircraft

echolocation (eh-koh-loh-KAY-shuhn)—the process of using sounds and echoes to locate objects

electrode (ih-LEK-trohd)—an object that conducts electricity

infrared (in-fruh-RED)—invisible waves of light that are usually given off by heat

larvae (LAR-vay)—insects at the stage of development between eggs and adults when they look like worms

paralyze (PAIR-uh-lize)—to make someone or something unable to move

predator (PRED-uh-tur)—an animal that hunts other animals for food

prey (PRAY)—an animal that is hunted and eaten by other animals

prow (PROW)—the front part of a boat or ship

radar (RAY-dar)—a device that uses radio waves to track the movement of objects

sonic (SON-ik)—having to do with sound waves

trait (TRATE)—a quality or feature of an animal or person

venom gland (VEN-uhm GLAND)—a body part some animals have that produces poison

Read More

Bell, Samantha. *Everyday Inventions Inspired by Nature.* Lake Elmo, MN: Focus Readers, 2019.

Cooke, Tim. *A Timeline of Military Robots and Drones.* North Mankato, MN: Capstone Press, 2018.

Miller, Tessa. *Fur & Claws: Technology Inspired by Animals.* Minneapolis: Lerner Publishing, 2018.

Internet links

Bombardier Beetle Escapes From a Toad
https://www.youtube.com/watch?v=54h1I9ykq8k

Boston Dynamics
https://www.bostondynamics.com/robots

Is That a Bug or a Robotic Spy?
https://www.roboticstomorrow.com/article/2017/12/is-that-a-bug-or-a-robotic-spy/11089/

Index

animals
    bats, 20
    bees, 22
    birds, 8, 10, 22, 24
    bombardier beetles, 13
    centipedes, 5
    dogs, 26
    dolphins, 9, 20
    dragonflies, 27
    electric eels, 16
    electric rays, 25
    falcons, 19
    fish, 20, 22
    grasshoppers, 13
    horses, 13
    insects, 20, 22
    mosquitoes, 18, 27
    moths, 22
    sharks, 9
    skunks, 14
    spitting spiders, 15
    tortoise beetle larvae, 12
    whales, 20
    whip scorpions, 14
Archytas, 6

biomimicry, 6, 7

echolocation, 20

infrared light, 18

radar, 19, 22
robots, 22, 27, 28
    SpotMini, 26
    micro aerial vehicles (MAVs), 27

sensors, 18, 24
Spartans, 12

vehicles, 6
    airplanes, 10, 19, 22
    ships, 9
    submarines, 18
    tanks, 5, 4, 13

wars
    Vietnam War, 20
    World War I, 4, 10
weapons
    bows and arrows, 6, 8, 28
    chemical weapons, 14–15
    drones, 22
    electric bullets, 25
    flamethrowers, 13
    Long Range Acoustic Device (LRAD), 21
    pepper spray, 15
    shields, 12
    Tasers, 16, 25
Wright brothers, 10